EAST BOSTON
THROUGH TIME

ANTHONY M. SAMMARCO
CONTEMPORARY PHOTOGRAPHS BY PETER B. KINGMAN

AMERICA
THROUGH TIME®
ADDING COLOR TO AMERICAN HISTORY

In memory of Gilda Pisapia Sammarco
and Marie Matarese Sammarco
Lovingly known as Auntie G and Auntie Chickie

East Bostonians by birth

Cover photograph: By the 1930s, Stevenson's Block at Meridian and Saratoga Streets in Central Square had Green's Furniture Store on the ground floor with Green's Hall above. On the right was the Seville Theater with its neon light marquee. The Seville Theater was designed by the Boston architectural firm Krokyn, Browne & Rosenstein and opened in 1930.

America Through Time is an imprint of Fonthill Media LLC
www.through-time.com
office@through-time.com

Published by Arcadia Publishing by arrangement with Fonthill Media LLC
For all general information, please contact Arcadia Publishing:
Telephone: 843-853-2070
Fax: 843-853-0044
E-mail: sales@arcadiapublishing.com
For customer service and orders:
Toll-Free 1-888-313-2665

www.arcadiapublishing.com

First published 2020

ISBN 978-1-63500-104-4

Typeset in Mrs Eaves XL Serif Narrow
Printed and bound in England

CONTENTS

Acknowledgments 4

Introduction 5

1 Maverick Square 9

2 Central Square 23

3 Day Square 33

4 Places of Worship 43

5 Schools 55

6 Transportation 65

7 A Neighborhood Called East Boston 77

8 Residences and Neighborhoods 87

John Fitzgerald Kennedy and Jacqueline Bouvier Kennedy walked in the Columbus Day Parade in East Boston in 1958, passing Santarpio's Pizza, founded by Frank Santarpio in 1903 as a bakery and serving pizza since the 1930s at Chelsea and Porter Streets. Kennedy was campaigning for reelection to the United States Senate and was greeted by cheering crowds as he and his wife walked in the parade. Kennedy's father, Joseph P. Kennedy, and paternal grandfather, Patrick J. Kennedy, all hailed from East Boston, so it was a welcoming home of a son of East Boston.

ACKNOWLEDGMENTS

I wish to especially thank Peter Bryant Kingman for his wonderful contemporary photographs of the East Boston neighborhood of Boston. He has captured the essence of the vintage photographs and has made this book not just an interesting compilation of the houses, businesses, squares and streetscapes of this historic neighborhood of Boston, but a visually fascinating one as well.

We wish to extend our sincere thanks and deep appreciation to:

Joel Andreasen; Marcos Barajas, Universal Church of the Kingdom of God; Jeanne Scaduto Belmonte; John Blundo; Boston City Archives, John McColgan; David Leonard, President Boston Public Library, Fine Arts, Sarah Hagen; Josephine Bruzzese; Michael Casamassima; Debra Cave and Jacopo Madaro; John Cecca, Jr.; Hutchinson and Pasqualina Cedmarco; Cesidio "Joe" Cedrone; the late Frank Cheney; Dr. John Christoforo; Edie Clifford; Congregational Library & Archives, Sara Trotta; Frank Conte; Dr. Edith DeAngelis; Ralph Dorato; East Boston Branch Boston Public Library, Margaret Kelly; East Boston Main Streets, Max Gruner; East Boston Museum and Historical Society; Kevin Farrell; Judge Joseph Ferrino; Robert Gibbons; Kathy Gillis; Harvard Divinity School, Andover-Harvard Theological Library; Bradley Jay, WBZ Radio 1030/iHeart Radio; Renata Kalnins; Jewish Heritage Center at the New England Historic Genealogical Society; Lee Cronin Kaitz; George Kalchev, Fonthill Media; Steve Kirk; Magdalena La Battaglia; Michael A. Laurano, East Boston's historian; Representative Adrian Madaro; Regina Marchi; Diane Modica; Elaine Moretti; Eddie Mulkern; Orleans Camera; Payne/Bouchier Fine Builders, Steve Payne and Oliver Bouchier; Steven M. Philbin; Lilian M.C. Randall; Francesca Ippolito Riley; Paul Rogers; Joe Ruggiero; Ron Scully; Steven Snyder; Alan Sutton, Fonthill Media; the late Sonny Tarbi; Dr. James Taylor; Lina Tramelli; George Williams; William Zarella.

All photographs are from the Archives & Special Collections of Healey Library, University of Massachusetts at Boston unless otherwise credited.

David Leonard
President, Boston Public Library

INTRODUCTION

> East Boston is noted for its ship-yards, foundries and sugar refineries. Here is the landing place of the Atlantic steamships, and the terminus of the Grand Junction Railway.
>
> Gazetteer of Massachusetts

Noddle's Island was named for William Noddle (1610-1632) and was one of the five islands off the coast of Boston. The largest of the islands, along with Hog's (later Breed's) Island, now referred to as Orient Heights, they represent modern day East Boston while Governor's, Apple and Bird Islands have been incorporated into Logan International Airport. Throughout the first two centuries after the Puritans settled Boston in 1630, the islands remained as pastureland used for the grazing of livestock and military fortifications.

However, in 1833 William Hyslop Sumner (1780-1861), one of the owners of Noddle's Island, formed the East Boston Company, a shareholding corporation, to oversee the residential and commercial development of the new neighborhood of East Boston. This was to be the first planned neighborhood of the nineteenth century (followed by the South End and Back Bay of Boston), with a grid of streets and squares that were laid out to create an urban neighborhood. The original plan envisioned four neighborhoods: Jeffries Point, Maverick Square, Central Square, and Eagle Hill. The irregular terrain of Hog's or Breed's Island (now Orient Heights) precluded the grid pattern being used and it would remain undeveloped until the turn of the twentieth century. To make the new neighborhood accessible, the East Boston Company established ferry service from Maverick Square to Rowe's Wharf in downtown Boston with the *Tom Thumb* and *Maverick* ferries, eventually including the *East Boston*, crossing the 132 rods of water. The developers also planned for the neighborhood to be composed of both residential as well as commercial development along with industries, and open land such as parks and East and West Wood Island, which were landscaped by Frederick Law Olmstead.

From eight residents in 1833, East Boston's population grew tremendously; by 1840 there were 1,455 residents and in 1865 there were 20,572 residents who moved here not just from the city, but also from surrounding towns, the New England states and the Canadian Maritimes. The attraction was not just a new neighborhood of Boston, but employment possibilities. By the 1840s, ship building and mercantile industries were to line the East Boston waterfront with prominent shipbuilders—among them Paul Curtis, who moved from Medford, and Donald McKay, who moved from Newburyport—who provided jobs, growth and stability and which made East Boston known throughout the United States as one of the foremost places for shipbuilding. Donald McKay, the designer of clipper ships, including the world-famous *Flying Cloud* (which in 1851 broke the established record for a voyage around Cape Horn), helped to create a steady hum in the shipyards, wharves, and warehouses which lined the waterfront. In 1839, Sir Samuel Cunard established his terminal for the London based *Cunard Line* in East Boston, and the ship RMS *Britannia* connected Boston to Liverpool, England. McKay's shipyard on Border Street thrived and one of his first commissions was to build five large clipper ships for Enoch Train's *White Diamond Line* between 1845 and 1850. McKay built the clipper ships *Washington Irving, Anglo Saxon, Anglo American, Daniel Webster*, and *Ocean Monarch*. Even after the age of clipper ships had passed, East Boston remained a mercantile center for immigration, shipping and marine repair.

William Hyslop Sumner wrote *A History of East Boston* in 1858, and it chronicled its early history as Noddle's Island through the creation of East Boston by the East Boston Company in 1833, and the tremendous growth over the next two decades. However, the "Father of East Boston" could hardly have envisioned the tremendous growth that would take place after the Civil War with not just residential and commercial development but a community that seemed to thrive on the cultural and ethnic diversity of its new residents. From the 1830s and 1840s when East Boston was largely settled by Yankees, it would attract Canadians, Irish, Jews from Germany and Eastern Europe, and Italians, who would become the major ethnic group of the neighborhood by 1920. With 23, 816 residents in 1870, by 1900 there were 43,478. Over the next century, the community seemingly developed as a thriving nexus of cultures, with many places of worship and places of entertainment and social clubs that began to define East Boston including the Golden Stairs in Jeffries Point.

Today, East Boston continues this long tradition of diversity and inclusion, and according to *Global Boston*, after the passage of the 1965 Immigration Act, opened a new era of immigration which augmented East Boston's population with a diverse grouping of immigrants:

> Beginning in the 1980s, a growing stream of Southeast Asians and Latin Americans began settling in the neighborhood. The largest groups came from Central America and Colombia ... Others were refugees from the Vietnam War and the Cambodian genocide. As they settled among the older and declining white population, some of them found a ... [mixed reaction to their arrival.]

Nevertheless, new arrivals continued to settle in Eastie in the 1990s and beyond, including newer groups from Mexico, Brazil, Peru, and Morocco.

With the influx of many diverse immigrants to East Boston in the late nineteenth and twentieth centuries, and a new and far more diverse wave of immigrants in the late twentieth century, the need for multi-family housing was tremendous. The formerly single-family houses were subdivided, and tenements were constructed in the older parts of the neighborhood. The housing would embrace the brick row houses of the 1840s, to wood three deckers and brick tenements that were built to house the new residents. The population would grow to 62,377 in 1915.

With the opening in 1904 of a tunnel for streetcars built under Boston Harbor to connect the city proper with East Boston, a distance of 132 rods by water, the ease of transportation at a nickel a ride literally transformed the neighborhood. This was the first underwater tunnel to be built in the United States, and was considered to be a marvel engineering fete. By the 1930s, the ascendancy of the automobile was a determining factor for a new way to connect the neighborhood to the city. Though carts and automobiles could use the ferries, a more convenient way was the Sumner Tunnel, which in 1934 was to be Boston Harbor's first auto crossing followed by the Callahan Tunnel in 1961. Eventually the Ted Williams Tunnel in 1995 linked East Boston with the Massachusetts Turnpike and South Boston. The East Boston Airfield opened in 1923 on the filled flats of Jeffries Point, and passenger service began in 1929. Landfill on Governor's and Apple Islands greatly expanded the airport in the 1940s, and in 1966 Wood Island Park was taken by eminent domain and developed as additional runway space. The airport operated under various city and state jurisdictions until the Massachusetts Port Authority was formed in 1959. Named the General Edward Lawrence Logan International Airport, the facility is one of the earliest municipal airports in the country and as the forty-eighth busiest airport in the world, it connects East Boston with points across the globe.

Today, East Boston is so much more than just Logan International Airport—it has become a destination that has evolved as a community that appreciates its rich and ever embracing history but also thrives on its reinvention. The creation of the Urban Wilds in 2016 was to protect "urban

wilds" in Boston's neighborhoods and to improve coastal habitats, rejuvenate fish populations, restore soil, and use for flood control and water quality improvement. The East Boston Greenway, which stretches from the wharves at Maverick Square to the Bayswater Urban Wild, has become a major addition to the neighborhood's green space and attractiveness as has Eastie Farm. However, Piers Park is one of the most attractive developments and is located on the west side of Maverick Square, overlooking Boston Harbor with panoramic views of the city. Designed by Pressley Associates Landscape Architects of Cambridge, the park was developed from the once thriving piers that had fallen into disuse and was redesigned as an accessible and attractive greenspace on the waterfront. Piers Park consists of multiple trails paved in brick and granite repurposed from the pier's original 1870 seawalls, native salt-tolerant plants, more than thirty-two tree varieties, seasonal flowers and ornamental shrubs and a 600-foot meandering brick pedestrian promenade with four smaller shade pavilions.

East Boston has been an extremely diverse neighborhood for well over a century and has the highest percentage of foreign-born residents of any Boston neighborhood. With a population that peaked at 64,000 in 1925, it has dropped to 42,000 today. Along with the construction of new buildings, condominiums, and the renovation of many apartment buildings in East Boston, the inevitable result is in the demand for higher rents, thereby forcing many longtime residents to leave the neighborhood. Now, with the influx of new residents, it has resulted in renewed interest in East Boston's historical housing stock, and many houses and buildings are being restored after years of neglect. It is hoped that the rich overlay of the wide spectrum of immigrants and their descendants will remain as a distinctive and contributing character of the neighborhood.

The vibrant neighborhood of East Boston features one of the most beautiful waterfronts in the city. Explore it through this visually beautiful book on *East Boston Through Time*, and then plan to visit and walk its streets and revel in its history, its architecture, and its open greenspace, and share in East Boston's rich diversity as a cultural melting pot.

1

Maverick Square

Maverick Square, seen in a lithograph by William S. Pendleton, showed the tremendous growth of East Boston in the two years since the East Boston Company began its residential and commercial development of the island in 1833. The Maverick House was opened in May of 1835 by the East Boston Company as the centerpiece of "Hotel Square" with the hotel boasting dining rooms, ball room, parlors, a reading room, and more than 100 other rooms offering "fish dinners and other jollifications." The *Maverick Coach* was a horse drawn omnibus, seen on the far left, which took passengers to the hotel from the ferries *Maverick* and the *Tom Thumb* as well as throughout the new neighborhood and onto Chelsea Beach where "surf bathing may be enjoyed in great perfection."

Maverick Square, named for early settler Samuel Maverick and seen in 1895, had a large oval green in the center with a tall flagpole, made from one of the discarded clipper ship wood masts from the McKay Shipyard on Border Street. The Sturtevant House, on the right, and Lyceum Hall and the East Boston Savings Bank, just to the right of the flagpole, were a major part of the growth and stability of East Boston and made Maverick Square the business center of the town. Today, this busy area is now referred to as Scarmella/ Maverick Square, in honor of Corporal Nicholas Scaramella of Co. D 301st Supply Train in World War I, and early settler Samuel Maverick.

Lyceum Hall in East Boston was located at Maverick Square and Sumner Street, and was originally the second edifice of the Maverick Congregational Church. Here in Sumner Hall, named for the Father of East Boston William Hyslop Sumner, learned lectures and other events were held for the edification of the local residents. These events were important in the development of adult education in America. During the mid-nineteenth century, hundreds of informal associations such as this one was established for the purpose of improving the social, intellectual, and moral fabric of society. On the corner was T. Arthur & Alley, a local pub, and to the right is the East Boston Savings Bank. Luongo's Restaurant on the ground floor of the building was destroyed by fire in 1942 with the deaths of six firefighters.

The Sturtevant House was built in 1858 by local entrepreneur and businessman Noah Sturtevant (1805-1861) on the site of the old Maverick House. An impressive five-story Italianate hotel, designed by William Washburn, with an iron arcaded ground floor and brick covered in mastic above, it had shops on the ground floor with reception rooms and a dining room for the hotel guests, many of whom stayed here on the night prior to their departure on the sailing lines located in East Boston that connected to Liverpool, England. Notice the stagecoach and the streetcar both stopped in front of the hotel. Demolished in 1927, this is the site of the East Boston Neighborhood Health Center.

The row of red brick houses was built in the 1840s between Meridian Street, on the left, and Chelsea Street facing Maverick Square. By the 1890s, though the houses were still residential, the ground floor of the house on the left had been remodeled for a bakery and Packard's Pharmacy, which had a large gilded mortar and pestle mounted on a pole and prominently displayed on the sidewalk. The street clock, on the left, was made by the E. Howard Clock Company in Roxbury, Massachusetts; notice the horse drawn barouche on the right.

Opened in December 1904, a tunnel had been built under Boston Harbor connecting the city proper with East Boston, a distance of 132 rods of water. Seen here in the early twentieth century, a streetcar emerges from the tunnel in Maverick Square. This was the first underwater tunnel to be built in the United States, and was considered to be a marvel engineering feat. By this time, the hotel was referred to as the Maverick House, and the Maverick House Exchange was on the ground floor corner of the hotel. Patrick Kennedy, father of Ambassador Joseph Kennedy and grandfather of President John Fitzgerald Kennedy, established a wine and spirits importing business here at the turn of the twentieth century. [*Courtesy of Frank Cheney*]

Maverick Square saw great alterations to the East Boston Tunnel in 1922 with the construction of the Maverick Square Station. The conversion of the tunnel from a trolley car operation to train operation transformed the line that would connect Scollay Square at Court Street in Boston and eventually Wonderland in Revere, Massachusetts, and henceforth be called the "Blue Line" of the Massachusetts Bay Transportation Authority. On the left is the Boston Sugar Refinery and on the right is the granite Winthrop Block with the First Ward National Bank and Bernie's Lunch. [*Courtesy of Frank Cheney*]

In the 1930s, a new station was built at Maverick Square for passengers traveling to the city or north towards Orient Heights or Revere Beach. This brick and concrete head house was to see residents pass through the doors throughout the day going to town for business or pleasure. The people standing in front have just emerged from the subway and are patiently waiting for buses to take them on to further points in East Boston, Chelsea, and Everett. [*Courtesy of Frank Cheney*

An obviously vocal Boston policeman has the distinct pleasure of directing vehicular traffic in Maverick Square. As the sign clearly states, "Keep Right—Two Way Traffic," however pedestrians, automobiles, trucks, and buses would, and still do, clog Maverick Square, either dropping off or picking up passengers or freight. On the right can be seen wood-framed houses with shops on the ground floor in the 1950s.

The street clock once in front of the Repino Memorial Home at 9 Chelsea Street was made by the E. Howard Clock Company in Roxbury, Massachusetts. Originally located in Scollay Square in front of the R. Marston & Company Dining Rooms at 23-29 Brattle Street in Boston's infamous West End entertainment district, it was salvaged in the late 1950s when the area underwent urban renewal and was re-erected in Maverick Square. The clock has been removed, but hopefully will be restored and re-erected.

Meridian Street (meridian meaning a line of longitude), which was laid out in 1833 and connects Maverick Square to Central Square and then onto the Chelsea line, had not just residences and churches but large numbers of commercial concerns. On the left is the Columbia Trust Company, which was founded in 1895 as the "people's bank." The *East Boston Leader* said that the bank's "birth was humble for its founders were men of limited means" but quickly became a major banking concern. Joseph P. Kennedy, following his graduation from Harvard University in 1912, served as president of the bank early in his career.

Designed by Edward Bowman Stratton, a well-known architect associated with Arthur H. Bowditch in the firm of Bowditch & Stratton, the Columbia Trust Company was an imposing and important banking institution in East Boston at the corner of Meridian and Maverick Streets. By 1970, the former Columbia Trust Company building had become the Fleet Bank, later the Shawmut Bank, and is today is the Santander Bank; next door is the East Boston Savings Bank, founded in 1848 and the present bank building built in 1913. On the left is the Three Corners Tobacco Shop.

The Rapino Memorial Home was at Chelsea and Maverick Streets in Maverick Square. Founded in 1927 by Anthony P. Repino, and later purchased by Benito "Benny" Tauro, a prominent local businessman who owned many businesses, but was perhaps best known as the owner of the former Rapino Funeral Homes in East Boston both in Maverick Square and in Orient Heights, which long served the neighborhood. The funeral home has been demolished and condominiums will be built on the site.

By 1970, the row of houses between Meridian and Chelsea Streets had been remodeled almost beyond recognition. Packard Pharmacy had modernized their signage and building facade, but the row house on the right was resurfaced with stucco and housed the popular Giovino's Café. Today, though the three row houses survive with a lack of zoning and preservation restrictions, many of the nineteenth-century buildings were, and still are, being altered beyond recognition.

2
Central Square

Central Square was laid out in 1833 by the East Boston Company as a large open area with an oval park in the center. Seen here in 1900, the mature trees in the park along Meridian Street all but obscure the Maverick Congregational Church of which only its spire is evident. The streets were laid with cobblestones and the walkways with flat granite pavers as pedestrian walkways. The streetcar seen in the center originated at Maverick Square and traveled along Meridian Street, terminating at Chelsea Square.

Central Square had a large oval park between Meridian Street and Border Street and had been planted with shade trees, which by the turn of the twentieth century had become so large that they created an oasis in the neighborhood. The area in the distance along Border Street was originally the Central Square Wharf Company, but was to be redeveloped in the 1960s by the Lombardo family, who created a shopping mall in Central Square. They began with a function hall known as Lombardo's Function Facility and later opened what is now called Liberty Plaza, the square's distinctly suburban strip mall. They expanded with a large supermarket, Liberty Market. The entrance to the Plaza features a small park, known as the Alfred L. Bertulli Park in honor of a local Marine killed in Vietnam in 1967.

The East Boston Masonic Hall was an impressive Italianate three-story building built in 1873 of brick and limestone trim with a dormered Mansard roof. The Grand Master of Masons in Massachusetts, the Most Worshipful Sereno Nickerson, formally dedicated the new Masonic Hall in Central Square. Hammatt Lodge, named for John B. Hammatt, with all the other Masonic groups, occupied these elegant quarters. On the ground floor were the Bennett Dry & Fancy Goods on the left, and the Boston One Price Clothing Store, and above, rented offices. The entire third floor was the masonic hall; Walcott & Company later purchased the building and a new Masonic Hall was built in 1892 at Meridian and Eutaw Streets, designed by Joseph Robbins.

Central Square, the junction of Meridian, Porter, Bennington, Saratoga, Border, and Liverpool Streets, seen in 1900, had both the remnants of red brick row houses on the far right, and large impressive commercial blocks such as the Stevenson's Block on the left, and on the right, the Walcott & Company, the Central Hat Company, and the Morrison Grocery Company; in 1931, this was replaced by a W. T. Grant Store. The spire on the upper right is that of the Saratoga Street Methodist Episcopal Church; notice the horse trough on the right for the watering of horses.

Stevenson's Block was an impressive red brick Queen Anne commercial building at 234-238 Meridian Street built by Joseph Stevenson (1838-1927,) a partner in the firm of A. G. & S. H. Whidden Shipwrights and Caulkers in East Boston, and later a well-known developer who built numerous residential and commercial structures in East Boston. At the turn of the twentieth century, the block housed the East Boston Post Office and the Knights of Columbus, as well as numerous dental offices on the upper floors.

By the 1930s, Stevenson's Block at Meridian and Saratoga Streets had Green's Furniture Store on the ground floor with Dr. Rubin's Dentist Office and Green's Hall above. On the right was the Seville Theater with its neon light marquee. The Seville Theater was designed by the Boston architectural firm Krokyn, Browne & Rosenstein and opened in 1930 as a Spanish-style theater that had a midnight blue ceiling with twinkling stars studded throughout and Italianate balconies; there was a large classical statue of the Venus de Milo set in a grotto in the lobby. Notice the kerosene lamps surmounting the stanchions in the foreground for evening traffic control.

Meridian Street, opposite Central Square, had many small shops including the F. W. Woolworth & Company 5 and 10 Cent Store, and Sonora next door, which later became Goldenberg's Department Store in the Meridian Block. The First Presbyterian Church, now La Luz Del Mundo, can be seen on the right. Today Walgreen's and its parking lot are on the site.

Meridian Street, looking towards Central Square, had numerous mothers with perambulators crowding the sidewalk in front of the F. W. Woolworth & Co store and the Meridian Block with Goldenberg's Store on the right, eagerly awaiting the morning opening. The three-story building on the left was Sabo Company, a popular men's and boy's outfitters store.

Meridian Street, with Havre Street on the right and popularly referred to as O'Shea's Corner, was a thriving crossroads with shops on the ground floor of former row houses that had been subdivided into apartments. The two streetcars provided ease of transportation and the horse-drawn delivery wagons brought fresh provisions to the shops. The sign on the left advertises "Everything to Furnish a Home" and J. A. O'Shea offered boots, shoes, and rubbers. Notice the First Presbyterian Church in the distance, all that survives from the older photograph.

The junction of Bennington, London, and Marion Streets was a combination of commerce and residential development. The street begins at Central Square as a narrow two-way road crowded with shops and houses and ends in Beachmont at Station Square, the intersection of Winthrop Street and State Road. On the left is a First National Store, in the center is now Peaches & Cream, the church on the right is the German Evangelical Lutheran Church (Immanuel Kirche), now the Central Assembly of God Church, and on the far right is the Renascent Variety Store, now Los Pinos.

3

DAY SQUARE

Looking from the roof of the Emerson School at Bennington and Prescott Streets in 1918, Day Square was a thriving crossroads west from Maverick and Central Squares. With a combination of residential housing and businesses, the area had grown tremendously since the turn of the twentieth century, as large-scale development of new houses that were being built at Orient Heights (seen on the upper right) would bring new residents. The Day Square Theater on the far left was designed by Nathan Douglas and built in 1913 as a photo play theater, now the site of Spinelli's. Notice the granite horse trough in the center of the square on the lower right.

Day Square is the intersection of Bennington and Chelsea Streets and has long been a thriving business district with stores, restaurants, and services. Day Square was named by the Boston Board of Aldermen on January 7, 1901, for Frederick W. Day, partner in F. B. Day & Son Apothecaries at Meridian and Saratoga Streets, who served as an Alderman on the Boston Common Council from 1899 to 1900. A granite memorial to him and the naming of Day Square in his memory was dedicated by the city in 1990. Seen in 1948, Day Square had the Modern Restaurant at the junction of the two streets, now known as Jeveli's, in the center, with a combination of small shops and residences on both sides of the street.

Looking east on Bennington Street at Day Square in 1948, the Modern Restaurant was on the ground floor of the three-story apartment building on the left. Opened by Pasquale Ievoli in 1924, the restaurant only seated about thirty people, but the restaurant was an immediate success as it served not only fine foods but the classic Italian dishes that it has become renowned for. Today, one of its most well know rooms is Jeveli's Terminal J Lounge, a pun on Logan International Airport.

Looking east on Chelsea Street in Day Square in 1948, Capitol Auto Parts and Machine Shop Service and a Colonial Esso Gasoline Station anchor the block leading to Shelby Street. Chelsea Street continues onto a stretch of gas tanks that line both sides of the street before one reaches Chelsea, Massachusetts. The gasoline company was a merger of two New England firms that were acquired by Standard Oil in the 1930s. They became Esso stations after the merger, but carried "Colonial" on the familiar Esso oval; today this is a Mobil Gas Station on the corner. On the right is the Modern Restaurant, in a 1903 multi-unit apartment building with interesting rounded pressed metal bays.

Chelsea Street at Day Square, between Prescott and Shelby Streets, had the Plaza Lounge, serving the popular Narragansett Beer which was founded in 1888 and was once the largest lager beer brewery in New England at one time; on the far left is the Plaza Lanes Bowling with the First National Super Market, which at one time was considered one of America's largest grocery chains and often had small neighborhood markets such as this one at Day Square. In 1983, Spinelli's Function Facility was founded by the Roberto Family, offering dining and catering for special occasions and parties and is an anchor in Day Square.

In 1924, Pasquale Ievoli, which was recorded as Jeveli when he arrived at Ellis Island, opened what is now Jeveli's Restaurant in East Boston. At the time, it only seated about thirty people, but the restaurant was an immediate success. Edmund Ievoli would work with his father in the early years and Louis "Lefty" Ievoli would work in the restaurant for most of his life. With the "Mediterranean Room," the "New Room" and the "Presidential Room," which was named in honor of United States President William Jefferson Clinton who dined at the restaurant in 1997, it is a popular place. Notice the billboard on the roof of the building that proclaims the "New Day Square—You'll Like the Difference."

Bennington Street, seen at Day Square, was laid out in 1834 and named for the Battle of Bennington during the American Revolution. It had a combination of three deckers and small shops between Chelsea and Bremen Streets. On the right is the Red Shutter, a popular lounge and dance hall, and on the left the Modern (Jeveli's) Restaurant.

Chelsea Street, looking west from Prescott Street, had many small shops that were the mainstay of Day Square including the Day Square Liquors, Dom Gambardella Insurance Agency, Consolidated Bookkeeping, and Prescott Cold Cuts and Sub Shop.

Looking inbound on Bennington Street, the area of Orient Heights (formerly known as Breed's Island) saw development in the early twentieth century with free standing wood three deckers being built as the housing of choice. As East Boston's population increased new areas were developed for housing and rather than free standing wood and brick houses such as at Jeffries Point and Eagle Hill, the new area of Orient Heights saw wood two-family houses and three deckers in the 1900-1930 period.

The Traffic Safety Island, seen on the right, was added to Bennington and West Brook Streets in 1948 to help control the increased automobile traffic, much of which emanated from the Sumner Tunnel and the Callahan Tunnel heading north, as well as the streetcars that ran the length of Bennington Street. With new street lighting, it was considered safer as the neighborhood grew.

4

PLACES OF WORSHIP

The Maverick Congregational Church, originally known as the First Congregational Church in East Boston, was the first place of worship to be established in East Boston. The Greek Revival church with four Doric columns supporting a pediment was built in 1837 on Maverick Street between London and Havre Streets; the congregation moved in 1844 to a Greek Revival church (later Lyceum Hall) at the corner of Sumner Street and Maverick Square, before settling into a larger Gothic Revival church in Central Square in 1875. In 1844, the church was sold to the Roman Catholics, who dedicated it under the patronage of St. Nicholas, who worshiped here until Most Holy Redeemer Church, seen on the left, was built in 1857 and this became the Sunday School and church library.

The Church of the Most Holy Redeemer was designed in the Gothic style of the thirteenth century by Patrick C. Keeley, the foremost Catholic architect in the United States, and built in 1857 at 72 Maverick Street. Founded in 1844 and dedicated to St. Nicholas, it was the first Roman Catholic church in East Boston, and it was renamed the Church of the Most Holy Redeemer when the Rockport granite church was built. From what was once a church built for a largely Irish Roman Catholic community, it today embraces a diverse community. Though its former 200-foot spire has been removed, the church is still an important anchor in the architecture of the Maverick Square neighborhood.

Our Lady of the Assumption Church, named for the Assumption of the Virgin Mary into Heaven, was designed in the Romanesque style by Patrick C. Keeley and built in 1869 on Sumner Street in Jeffries Point. The red brick church had recessed arches with narrow stained-glass windows, a heavily bracketed cornice, and an imposing 126-foot bell tower, which was removed in 1947. The Italianate cottage on the right, which served as the Rectory, was also designed by Keeley with unique bonnet dormers surmounting triple windows, but was replaced by a red brick rectory in the late 1940s.

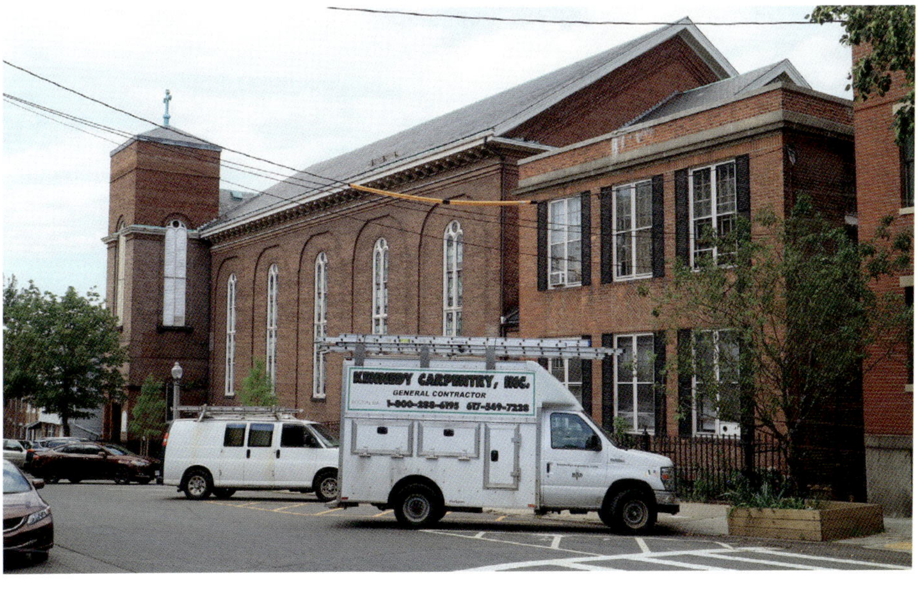

The Saratoga Street Methodist Episcopal Church was built at 10 Saratoga Street in 1865. An elegant church with columns supporting a façade pediment with an octagonal belfry, it had a thriving congregation in the nineteenth century. The church would merge with the Meridian Street Bethel in 1917 to form Union Chapel, and the church was then was used by St. Paul's Italian Methodist Episcopal Church, which was organized in 1920 by Giovanni Orro. The church would federate in 1948, joining with St. John's Episcopal and the Congregational Society, but was disbanded in 1956 with the death of Rev. Gaetano Iorrizo, the pastor. This is now the site of Central Park Lanes Bowling Center.

The First Presbyterian Church in East Boston was designed as a Victorian Gothic church and built in 1870 at 130 London Street near Central Square. The congregation was founded in 1853, worshiping in a wood-framed church that was destroyed by fire in 1870. This high-Victorian Gothic church was constructed in 1870 and once had an impressive spire that was removed in the 1950s. The church was closed 1996 and today two congregations worship here: Iglesias del Dios Vivo and La Luz del Mundo, which reflects the diversity of the neighborhood in the last few decades.

The Church of the Sacred Heart was designed by John H. Besarick as a wood Gothic Stick Style church and was formally dedicated on the Feast of the Sacred Heart in 1874 by Archbishop Williams at the corner of Brooks and Paris Streets. In 1965, a fire destroyed the church, however, through the dedication of parishioners, the church was rebuilt in 1966 and has continued to flourish. Today, with churches being closed, Sacred Heart Parish has welcomed the parishioners of St. Mary Star of the Sea Parish and Our Lady of Mt. Carmel Parish and is now "a multi-ethnic, socially, culturally, and educationally diverse faith community" worshiping in a modern church.

The Maverick Congregational Church was designed as a high style Gothic Revival church and was built in 1875 at Central Square South. This is the oldest religious society in East Boston, having been founded in 1836. The Gothic Revival church was said at the time to be a "large and imposing structure of brick, and stands commandingly in Central Square." Today the East Boston Social Center is on the site of the church. In the mid-twentieth century, the Maverick and Baker Congregational Churches merged to form Baker-Maverick Congregational Church, and then merged again with the two Episcopal parishes of St. John's and St. Andrew's, completing the merger in 1949. Today the church is known as Grace Church Federated, located at 760 Saratoga Street.

St. John's Episcopal Church was designed by Wallis Howe of Martin and Hall Architects and built in 1903 at 80 Lexington Street. Howe designed the church in the Elizabethan Gothic Revival style with red brick and limestone detailing with two octagonal crenelated towers flanking the façade and a monumental stained-glass window on the façade. The church was said to be of "working people, by working people, for working people grateful for the gifts which have come to it so richly in recent years." The East Boston APAC Headstart has used the former church for many years as its headquarters.

The Church of Our Father was organized in 1845 at Richie Hall. This church was designed by Sheperd S. Woodcock, once in partnership with George Meacham, and built in 1867 at the corner of Meridian and Havre Streets and was said to be "one of the handsomest and one of the most costly structures of East Boston." The church was the only Unitarian church in East Boston and was organized "to diffuse the knowledge and promote the interests of pure Christianity." The church was sold in 1900 and the congregation moved to 85 Marion Street where they erected a new church. The site is today the East Boston Post Office with other small shops.

Temple Ohel Jacob was East Boston's oldest and largest synagogue, located on the corner of Paris and Gove Streets. Ohel Jacob was founded in 1893 as the first place of worship for Jews as there were large numbers of Jews moving to East Boston in the early twentieth century. With an estimated 5,000 Jews in East Boston in 1910, the congregation built a new synagogue on the site in 1905, which was destroyed by fire in 1973. As the Jewish community grew, so did the need for synagogues, and by 1913 there were at least four others in East Boston: Beth David, Linath Hazedek, Keser Israel, and Choreh Mismaeth. The first Jewish cemetery in New England was opened in 1844 by Temple Ohabei Shalom of Boston on Wordsworth Street.

The Church of St. Mary Star of the Sea was founded in 1864 at 63 Moore Street as a "neat, though unpretentious building," with a small belfry, and was located at the furthest end of East Boston on Breed's Island (Orient Heights) adjoining Chelsea and Winthrop, Moore Street having been extended in 1881. A new cruciform buff brick church was designed by Franz Joseph Untersee and built in 1910 due to the dramatic increase in the number of Roman Catholics moving into the neighborhood. Untersee was a prominent architect who in 1910 built the twin spires on the Mission Church, the Basilica and Shrine of Our Lady of Perpetual Help. Today this is known as the Universal Church of the Kingdom of God.

Our Lady of Mount Carmel was named for the Blessed Virgin Mary in her role as patroness of the Order of the Brothers of the Blessed Virgin Mary of Mount Carmel. The red brick and limestone Craftsman style church at 120 Gove Street was built in 1907 by Italian immigrants who were the artisans and carpenters and bricklayers and stone cutters, and it was they who built this church in which to worship with their own hands. The church was suppressed by the Archdiocese of Boston in 2004; Frankfort Gove LLC has proposed turning the former church site on Gove and Frankfort streets into two buildings, with 115-unit condominiums.

5
SCHOOLS

The first school in East Boston was opened in 1837 at Meridian and Emmons Streets and was known as the Lyman School in honor of Theodore Lyman (1792-1849,) the fifth mayor of Boston. Lyman was graduated from Harvard College and served as mayor from 1834 to 1836 and was a strong advocate of the East Boston Company that laid out the grid plan for the new neighborhood. He was also a benefactor of the Massachusetts Horticultural Society and was the founder of the State Reform School for Boys. By the late 1860s, the tremendous increase in population in East Boston required new schools. The old Lyman School became the first branch of the Boston Public Library, the first branch in the United States. This same building also served for the East Boston District Court.

The second Lyman School was designed by Bryant and Rogers and built in 1869 at 30 Gove Street; after a fire in 1871, the school was rebuilt. Gridley J. Fox Bryant and Louis P. Rogers were among the most prominent architects in Boston at the time and Bryant was the architect of the Old City Hall, Boston City Hospital and the Charlestown State Prison. In the early 1900s, the school also offered evening vocational classes for immigrants. Today, known as the Lyman School Apartments, the former school building was repurposed in 2016 to create forty-five units of housing for the elderly and disabled.

The Emerson School was named for Ralph Waldo Emerson (1803-1882), an essayist, poet, and founder of *The Atlantic*, but probably best known for his contributions to the transcendentalist movement. He graduated from Harvard College and the Harvard Divinity School and preached at Boston's Second Church. Emerson served on the Boston School Committee in the early 1830s and the three-story red brick Italianate school at the corner of Bennington and Prescott Streets near Day Square was named in his honor, as a man universally respected and beloved by Bostonians.

The Chapman School was named for Jonathan Chapman (1807-1848), the eighth mayor of Boston, serving from 1840 to 1842. A graduate of Phillips Exeter and Harvard College, he studied law under Judge Lemuel Shaw and was not just an attorney, but a literary contributor to the *North American Review*. He was also an advocate of the establishment of the Cunard Lines steamship service between East Boston and Liverpool, England. The school was designed by Greenleaf and Cobb and built in 1901 on Eutaw Street.

The Curtis Guild School was named for Curtis Guild (1860-1915), governor of Massachusetts from 1905 to 1907. A graduate of Harvard College, he was the owner and editor of the *Boston Commercial Bulletin*, a newspaper pertaining to the wool brokerage business. Well respected as a politician, he served as Ambassador Extraordinary and Plenipotentiary to Russia from 1911 to 1913. The school was designed by Harrison H. Atwood and built in 1921 at 5 Ashley Street.

The Hugh Roe O'Donnell School was named for Father O'Donnell, a native of Dublin and a descendant of Aodh Ruadh Ó Domhnaill; he served as pastor of the Church of St. Mary Star of the Sea and was an advocate for East Boston. Designed by the Department of School Buildings, the school was built in 1932 at 33 Trenton Street. Today, the Hugh Roe O'Donnell School states that it "is a safe, successful, high-performing and family-friendly school ... welcomes students of all ethnicities, and we recognize and celebrate the deep cultural diversity that the O'Donnell School represents."

The John B. Cashman School was designed by the City of Boston Department of School Buildings and built in 1931 on Paris Street. The school was named for Senator John B. Cashman (1886-1928), who had served in the Massachusetts House of Representatives from East Boston from 1918 to 1922, and later in the Massachusetts Senate from 1925 to 1928. A native born son, he was one of ten children of John and Bridget Barry Cashman and the husband of Charlotte F. Bowman, to whom he was married in 1920.

The Donald McKay School was designed by Charles Reggio Greco and built in 1926 at 122 Cottage Street. The school was named for Donald McKay (1810-1880), a noted clipper ship designer who opened his shipyard in 1844 on Border Street in East Boston. McKay built some of the fastest clipper ships and one of his first commissions was to build five large packet ships for Enoch Train's *White Diamond Line* between 1845 and 1850. McKay built the clipper ships *Washington Irving*, *Anglo Saxon*, *Anglo American*, *Daniel Webster*, and *Ocean Monarch*. The *Flying Cloud*, built in 1851, made two eighty-nine-day passages New York to San Francisco. In 1869, McKay sold his shipyard and retired to a farm in Hamilton, Massachusetts.

The East Boston High School, organized in 1880 as a branch of the English and Girls' High Schools, was designed by John Lyman Faxon and built in 1901 at 127 Marion Street. In 1926, the school was renamed the Joseph H. Barnes School, in honor of the man who organized Company K of the 129th Regiment of Massachusetts Volunteers in the Civil War, when the present high school was built; an addition was designed by Charles Reggio Greco and built in 1933. An impressive Renaissance Revival design faced in yellow brick and limestone, the school was added to the National Register of Historic Places in 2006. Today, the school has been repurposed as the Barnes School Apartments for the elderly and disabled.

The East Boston High School was designed by the John M. Gray Company of Boston and built in 1926 at the corner of White and Brooks Streets on Eagle Hill, the former site of the East Boston Reservoir. In 2000, Cole and Goyette Architects renovated the school adding a new gymnasium with bleachers, offices, locker rooms with showers, a faculty dining area, and a school kitchen, new engineering systems, technology network, accessibility, and site improvements. Today, the high school has a professional partnership with the Harvard University Graduate School of Education's Teacher Education Program and in 2016, the school was designated as an Historical Landmark.

6

TRANSPORTATION

Seen from the Boston wharves, the ferry *Ben Franklin* leaves the North Ferry Slip at Rowe's Wharf headed across Boston Harbor for East Boston in 1899. The workers in the foreground from E. A. Clark Artesian & Driven Wells Company are on a small barge and are making test borings for the proposed East Boston Tunnel, which would connect Court Square in Boston with Maverick Square in East Boston, a distance of 132 rods of water. The East Boston Tunnel was opened in 1904 as a streetcar tunnel, and the ease and low cost of transportation was a major factor in East Boston's tremendous population growth. [*Courtesy of Frank Cheney*]

The Boston, Revere Beach & Lynn Railroad, fondly known as the Narrow Gauge Railroad, was laid from East Boston to Lynn, Massachusetts, and Engine 10, built by the Mason Machine Works, exits a tunnel. Completed in 1875 in conjunction with the establishment of the new ferry line, this railway, including a 400-foot-long tunnel under Webster Street in Jeffries Point, allowed passengers to travel with relative ease between Lynn and East Boston, and then connect to Boston via ferry at the South Ferry Slip. A second, adjacent tunnel was added in 1894. [*Courtesy of Frank Cheney*]

The Boston, Revere Beach & Lynn Railroad followed the coastline north-eastward through the resort of Revere Beach to the terminus at Lynn, and there was a branch split at Orient Heights to a loop through Winthrop. Popularly known as the Narrow Gauge, this train heads southwest approaching the Orient Height Station. Notice the row of billboards with the wood three deckers on the east side of the railway bed and the houses on Orient Heights. [*Courtesy of Frank Cheney*]

Two streetcars, the one on the left arriving from Meridian Street and the other from Chelsea Street, enter the decline of the new East Boston Tunnel that went under Boston Harbor and connected Maverick Square with Court Square in Boston. On the far left is a corner of the Winthrop Savings Bank and in the center are red brick row houses that had been built in the 1840s, but converted to shops by the early twentieth century.

Streetcar 2057 is seen on Lexington Street in 1898, connecting the North Ferry slip in East Boston with Lexington Street. This open-air streetcar with striped awnings and wood slat seats was built by J. M. Jones Company in 1889 and was a pleasant summer ride through the neighborhood. This streetcar was eventually sold in 1910 to the Aroostook Valley Railroad in Maine. [*Courtesy of Frank Cheney*]

Streetcar 2067 emerges from Cottage Street onto Sumner Street at Jeffries Point in 1905 as it crosses the tracks of the Grand Junction Railroad, which was a short line chartered in 1847 that connected the East Boston waterfront to the Boston & Maine. The railroad crossing sign clearly warns to "Look for the Engine." Notice the houses on either side of Sumner Street—on the left they are red brick row houses and on the right, wood row houses. The spire seen in the distance is that of the Our Lady of the Assumption Church.

Streetcar 5061 is seen on Sumner Street in Jeffries Point in 1915, having come from the tunnel at Maverick Square. The duplex house in the center is 496-502 Sumner Street and it faces McCormick Square. Notice the horse-drawn wagon of the New England Telephone and Telegraph Company on the right. The newfangled telephone, a rarity even in 1915, was invented by Alexander Graham Bell and would eventually become the American Bell Telephone Company. [*Courtesy of Frank Cheney*]

Streetcars 5368 and 7013 are seen at the intersection of Bennington and Leyden Streets in 1937. Gladstone Street was laid out in 1886 and connects Walley Street (formerly Washburn Avenue) to Route 1A North in Orient Heights. The street was named for William Ewart Gladstone (1809-1898) who was a British statesman and Liberal Party politician; in a career lasting six decades, he served as Prime Minister of the United Kingdom. [*Courtesy of Frank Cheney*]

Bennington Street, looking towards Central Square in 1948 with numerous automobiles, had both residences as well as stores and the Central Square Theater, seen on the right. Built in 1930 between Central Square and Marion Street, it was a popular theater in the neighborhood with a large chevron marquee with the theater's name in big letters on the front and sides and the theater could seat 1,100 moviegoers. Later, Starlight Bowling Alleys were located here. On the right was Pericola's Rexall Drugstore, Butter's Furniture Company, Kennedy Butter & Eggs, and the Ideal Market. [*Courtesy of Frank Cheney*]

Originally called the East Boston Airport, it opened in 1923 with funds from the Massachusetts Legislature that were matched by the Boston Chamber of Commerce, and the airport was primarily used by the Massachusetts Air Guard and the Army Air Corps. The tiny airfield was built by the United States Army and was 189 acres where the first airplane, piloted by Lieutenant Kitchell Snow, touched down on June 13, 1923, on a 1,500-foot cinder runway. This is the Administration Building, and notice the biplane surmounting the control tower. In 1943, a new and expanded airport was renamed in honor of Major General Edward Lawrence Logan (1875-1939), a state senator and presiding judge at the South Boston Municipal Court.

As early as the 1830s, ferries were used to cross Boston Harbor to East Boston with the *Maverick* and *Noddle Island* providing passenger and freight transportation from "sunrise till 12 o'clock at night." The East Boston Company saw tremendous residential growth through the ferries and the population rose from 1,455 in 1840 to 20,572 in 1865. Seen here, the *Governor Russell*, named for Governor William Eustis Russell, provided not just passenger transport but also horse-drawn wagons, seen on the rear deck. Among the ferries in the early twentieth century were the *Noddle Island, Newtown, Brewster, Dartmouth,* and *Ashburnham*. The contemporary photograph shows the *Frederick L. Nolan Jr.* of the Boston Harbor Cruise Line.

The Sumner Tunnel, seen looking towards Porter Street, was opened on June 30, 1934, and had toll booths that charged a toll for automobiles to enter or exit the underwater tunnel; the tunnel initially carried traffic going in both directions until 1961. Named for William Hyslop Sumner, the Father of East Boston, it opened in 1934 and carried traffic in both directions until the opening of the parallel Callahan Tunnel, which opened in 1961 and was named for William F. Callahan, who was killed in World War II.

7

A Neighborhood Called East Boston

The East Boston Memorial Stadium, now called Sartori Stadium in honor of Judge James Sartori of the East Boston District Court, was built by the Massachusetts Department of Public Works in 1951 at 150 Porter Street near Logan Airport. It had an amusement park and athletic facilities for children, including a wading pool, a football field, a baseball diamond, tennis courts, and a gym. CBI Architects recently evaluated the existing conditions of the stadium adjacent to Logan Airport, and the 4,300-seat concrete grandstand structure was fully renovated, including concession stands, locker rooms, and toilet facilities underneath the grandstand.

Founded in the 1880s, the Immigrants Home offered financial relief and social services for newly arrived immigrants at the port of East Boston. The five-story building is at 72 Marginal Street and was built in 1912; the building later became *Landfall*, the first senior citizens housing in East Boston. Today, it has elderly housing and an office for the East Boston Development Corporation. Nearby was the East Boston Immigration Station, at 285 Marginal Street, which was constructed as a processing and detention facility for immigrants arriving in Boston. It operated from 1920 to 1954, and was demolished in 2011.

The Boston City Hospital East Boston Relief Station was designed by Edward Percy Dana and built in 1907 at 14 Porter Street. Under the auspices of Boston City Hospital, it offered ten beds for patients and staffed doctors and nurses that spoke Yiddish and Italian, the predominant language of the new residents; the hospital was closed in 1938. In the 1970s, Conexions was located here, offering help to those struggling with the use and abuse of and addiction to chemical substances. Today, the North Suffolk Mental Health Association is located here.

The East Boston Court House was designed by the architectural firm of McLaughlin and Burr, partners James E. McLaughlin and G. Houston Burr, as a chased Classical Revival building, and dedicated in 1931. Located at 37 Meridian Street, it replaced the first courthouse that was originally located at the first Lyman School, which also housed the East Boston Branch, Boston Public Library, and the East Boston Courthouse at Meridian and Paris Streets. Today, the court serves East Boston, Winthrop, Logan Airport, and the Sumner and Callahan Tunnels.

This East Boston Branch Boston Public Library building was built in 1914 in the Classical Revival style and designed by James E McLaughlin of McLaughlin and Burr at 280-282 Meridian Street. East Boston has the great claim to fame having the first municipally supported branch of a library in the world. A new branch library was opened in 2013 in an architecturally innovative building and award-winning design by William Rawn Associates Architects, and is located on Bremen Street.

The George Robert White Health Unit was designed by Abbott, Coolidge, Shepley, and Bulfinch and built in 1924 at 79 Paris Street. George Robert White (1847-1922) was the owner of the Potter Drug and Chemical Company that manufactured Cuticura Soap, an antibacterial medicated soap, and he was a great philanthropist whose bequest to the city of Boston was to be used "for creating works of public utility and beauty." The health center in East Boston was the second to be built in Boston through his largess. Today, this is the East Boston Neighborhood Health Center.

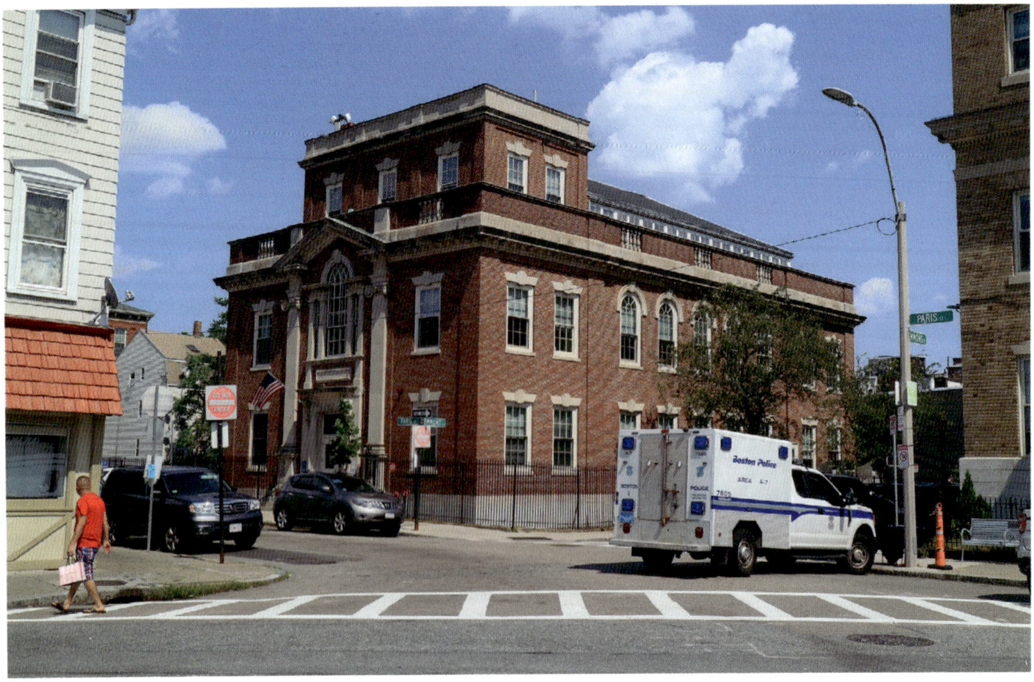

Designed by architects Harrison H. Atwood and Charles J. Bateman, Boston City Architects, this yellow brick fire house was built in 1891 at 60 Paris Street. The firehouse was built on the site of a previous firehouse that had been constructed in 1851 and occupied by a hand-pulled apparatus. Engine 9 and Ladder 2 remained in this firehouse until May 13, 1977, when the firehouse was closed and the building became the Italian American War Veterans Post 6.

Trinity Neighborhood House was originally the Noah Sturtevant House and built in 1844 at 406 Meridian Street. In 1917, it became the Trinity Neighborhood House and Day Nursery, a settlement house program originally established by Trinity Church rector Phillips Brooks in 1881 and operated as a social service center of Trinity Church. Caroline Orr became the director of the settlement house, and the children she mentored had a variety of experiences in nature, arts and crafts, music, dancing, reading, and field trips. Today, the building is owned by Neighborhood of Affordable Housing, Inc. and is a sixteen-unit single-resident occupancy facility for the formerly homeless.

The Orient Palace Theatre was built in 1922 at 985 Bennington Street in Orient Heights. The theater boasted a rectangular marquee, the design of which was said to be influenced by a Beijing Imperial Palace roof line and had an Art Deco facade. The Orient Palace had presented MGM films and had 820 seats and was a considered a favorite neighborhood movie house. Seen here in 1953 the movie *Dangerous When Wet* was being shown. Today this is the New Saigon Restaurant.

The Madonna, Queen of the Universe statue arrived at the Don Orion Home from Rome in large wood crates and would be erected in front of Don Orion before being placed within a shrine, rather than surmounting the stone parapet as originally intended, as due to the immense height of the statue, it might interfere with airplanes landing or taking off from Logan International Airport. Designed by Italian sculptor Arrigo Minerbi, it was inspired by the *Modonna Salus Populi Romani* in Rome, and the Madonna National Shrine was dedicated in 1954 on Orient Avenue in Orient Heights.

8

Residences and Neighborhoods

Neptune Road was a charming tree-lined street, with three deckers that connected Bennington Street and the entrance to Wood Island, renamed World War Memorial Park in the 1920s; this was a waterfront park designed by Frederick Law Olmsted in the late nineteenth century. An elegant street with a center island, *The Boston Globe* referred to the street as a "miniature Commonwealth Avenue." In the early 1970s, families lost their homes by eminent domain along Neptune Road, and as Logan Airport expanded, planes flew in low over the residential blocks and conflicts with airport officials escalated. Wood Island Park was leveled early one morning in 1967 and two years later workmen with chain saws toppled the elm trees along the road.

Looking down Sumner Street from Seaver Street in Jeffries Point, which was named for Dr. John Jeffries (1796-1876), the trees that had been set out in the 1840s through the generosity of William Hyslop Sumner and Noah Sturtevant created a shady oasis in the summer months at the turn of the twentieth century. On the right is the spire of the Our Lady of the Assumption Church. As the *Gazetteer of Massachusetts* states, "By 1879 there were 17 miles of streets [in East Boston.] These, from the first, have uniformly been named for our own country towns and eminent men."

Built in the 1840s, 222 Webster Street is an impressive red brick duplex house; the two houses were remodeled for the Jeffries Point Branch of the Boston Public Library after it outgrew its previous library space on Webster Street opposite Belmont Square (now Brophy Memorial Park). The branch library closed during the 1950s and the building was remodeled as a two-family house with a prominent entrance, and remains as such today. Notice the Italianate Mansard roof house on the right dating from the early 1870s.

Belmont Park, once the site of Fort Strong and now known as Brophy Memorial Park in memory of Michael J. Brophy (1881-1936) who served as a member of the House of Representatives, was laid out in 1833 as an open tree-lined park between Seaver, Sumner, Webster and Lamson Streets, but much smaller than Maverick or Central Squares. The Jeffries Point neighborhood surrounding the park became a very desirable place to live, with most residential development occurring between 1840 and the early twentieth century. In the center is the Jeffries Point Branch Boston Public Library, and to the left the row house of John H. Sullivan, president of the Columbia Trust; on the right are red brick swell bay facade row houses, which were similar to those being built in Boston's South End in the 1840s.

The mansion facing Monmouth Square was once the home of Governor John Lewis Bates (1859-1946) who served on Boston's Common Council, and was then elected to the Massachusetts House of Representatives in 1893, serving in that body until 1899. From 1897 to 1899, he was Speaker of the House; he was elected governor serving from 1903 to 1905. Bates worked to promote East Boston, securing legislative approval of the first tunnel under Boston Harbor, joining the neighborhood to the rest of the city. The mansion was later used by Dr. James H. Strong as the Strong Hospital from 1920 to the 1950s. On the right is the All Souls Universalist Church, designed by local architect Joseph S. Eastman and built in 1890; today the White Street Baptist Church and the Iglesias Cristiana Nueva Vida both worship here.

Donald McKay's House was built in 1844 at 80 White Street on the crest of Eagle Hill. McKay was one of the preeminent shipbuilders in the nineteenth century with his shipyard being located on Border Street. He built this high style Greek Revival mansion on Eagle Hill and he incorporated thirteen pilasters on the flat-roofed porch on the west side of his house, which were said to honor the thirteen original colonies. The dining room is oval in shape and said "to look like a ship." The McKay House was designated a Boston Landmark by the Boston Landmarks Commission and is listed in the National Register of Historic Places.

17 Princeton Street was a freestanding wood Italianate row house built in 1863. The medical office of Dr. Carlista Stone was on the first floor and she lived above. The house is three stories in height with a projecting two-story bay (with Dr. Stone seen sitting in the second-floor window) and a Mansard roof with projecting dormers. It was an attractive house similar to those being built for the burgeoning middle class, who were settling in East Boston just after the Civil War.

Lexington Street, named for the Battle of Lexington during the American Revolution, was laid out to connect Meridian and East Eagle Street. A streetcar travels along the elm tree lined street as it passes a row of small wood houses between 108 and 116 Lexington Street. These fairly identical houses, with a small porch and a single window in the pedimented façade, date to the late nineteenth century and created an attractive streetscape, along with a convenient streetcar that connected to Maverick Square and then on to Boston.

Known locally as the "Wedding Cake House," this high style duplex three decker is at 373 Meridian Street; with paired Ionic Columns, modified Palladian windows and a projecting third floor oriel, it is lavish in its Colonial Revival details. On the right is 388 Meridian Street, with an eagle connoting "Eagle Hill" carved into the pediment above the front porch. Three deckers were an architectural style that began at the turn of the twentieth century, built of wood and usually freestanding with porches and apartments with running water. They proliferated Boston and were built in every neighborhood.

By the early twentieth century, Orient Heights had been laid out for residential development and had large single, two-family and three decker houses being built with proximity to the ocean. Orient Heights was originally one of the five islands that comprised East Boston prior to its development by the East Boston Company, and was named for Boston's trade with China in the nineteenth century. The curvilinear streets, many with ocean views, included Ford Street, seen here looking towards Breed Street in 1915. The brick duplex three decker on the left from 1907 and the wood three decker on the right, and those being built on Antrim Street, are typical of the neighborhood.